# PRAISE FOR OVERCOMING

In this compact volume, Dr. Diana Bowling melds elegant poetry with highly empathic psychodynamic psychotherapy. This enriching expression of therapeutic process in poetic form exudes strength, hope, humanity, and beauty.

—Gerald Amada, Ph.D., author of *Professor Kittleman's Therapy* and *A Guide to Psychotherapy*

The ability to shed light on the often mysterious workings of therapy and make them less frightening and maybe even more inviting is quite an accomplishment. To do so, therapists carry on a never-ending internal dialogue: What is happening with my client? What is happening with me? How do I separate those processes while at the same time melding them together to get where my client wants to be? Diana Bowling captures for us the delicate balance of being deeply aware of but also unobtrusive to a client. She shows us how catching the words and feelings offered, turning them into something useful, or helpful, or insightful is a dance of giving and receiving. She gives; her patient receives, and visa versa. In the poetic offerings of *Overcoming*, she gives; her readers receive.

—Sarah SJ Guck, LCSW, MDiv

Dr. Bowling's prose poems are written with an exceptional economy of language. Her unique presentation of the therapeutic process through poetry grants the reader access into what for many is a mysterious world. One can sense the early hesitancy of the patient's self-disclosure and the generous openness of the therapist. The rhythm of healing is slowly revealed session after session. As trust expands, the patient seems more accustomed to vulnerability and is freer to share, more deeply, the history and secrets that were the sources of pain, and finally, to embrace the forgiveness and confidence needed to move forward in life.

—Lorraine Rose, MS Ed., author, published poet, *Praise the Rain* and recipient of long-term therapy

More than a book of poems, *Overcoming* explores our humanness through poetry—our fears and failures and losses and epiphanies—and then pairs poetry with insight into psychological process. This collection both circles the human experience of healing and puts a fine point on it. It's both intimate and clinical, a nuanced insight into what it means to be alive, to blossom into ourselves.

—Rosemerry Wahtola Trommer,
author of *Hush* and *Naked for Tea*

In this poetic series of exchanges between patient and therapist, Dr. Bowling has managed to convey the rhythms, tones, themes, and feelings of the therapeutic relationship—a truly masterful accomplishment. In my career as a therapist, I experienced it as a dance of sorts, in which the therapy sessions reflected the intricate steps – sometimes forward and sometimes back—that the therapeutic relationship takes over time, gently allowing the patient to move toward healing, self-knowledge, and growth. As I read Dr. Bowling's poems, memories of 40 years of conversations with my patients came flooding back to me, reminding me of tentative but incredibly brave first sessions; individual journeys from grief or rage or guilt to healing, cathartic moments of self-discovery, and then tentative steps toward resolution and separation from the therapeutic relationship. Our patients remain part of us, as we do of them, and Dr. Bowling's poetry reflects the deeply personal yet professional ties that allow growth to occur in patients as well as their therapists. I encourage anyone who considers becoming either a therapist or a patient, or who simply wants to witness the power of the therapeutic relationship, to read this artful description of the art that is psychotherapy.

—Rosalind Kalb, PhD, Clinical Psychologist

Mercury HeartLink
www.heartlink.com

# OVERCOMING

To Maggie —

I hope you find meaning
in your journey through
this book.

Regards,
Diana Bowling

# OVERCOMING

*Poems about Psychotherapy*

Diana Bowling, PhD

Mercury HeartLink

Copyright ©2021 Diana Bowling, PhD

ISBN 978-1-949652-14-7
ISBN: 978-1-949652-16-1 (hardcover)
ISBN: 978-1-949652-15-4 (e book)
Publisher: Mercury HeartLink
Silver City, New Mexico
Printed in the United States of America

Author photo by Meghan Morin
Painting of the author by Sarah Bowling
Layout and cover design by Denise Weaver Ross

Mercury HeartLink: consult@heartlink.com

Mercury HeartLink
www.heartlink.com

# PREFACE

This book of poems came about in response to years of friends, family members, and acquaintances asking me what it is like to be a clinical psychologist. Many ask about the toll it takes and if it is depressing to listen to people's problems all day. Others wonder if boredom or impatience prevail when individuals are stuck and there is no observable progress or change. Others ask about the different types of psychotherapy and theoretical orientations. Generally, I find my responses lacking as I try to describe working with patients in long-term, psychodynamic psychotherapy. I talk about it being an open-ended process, a depth approach rather than a more targeted, problem-solving approach. Eyes glaze or there is nervous laughter. The conversation finds traction when I allow myself to speak freely about the rewarding nature of psychotherapy. I talk about being with people in a process of change that is positive and enduring.

I have learned that this conversation takes time. I find it impossible to respond with succinct brevity to casual inquiries about psychotherapy. This streamlined approach devalues the complexity and nuance inherent in the process of change. Even with ample time, I am struck repeatedly by how difficult it is to describe what goes on in psychotherapy, how the enduring emotional and behavioral change I speak of is achieved. Poetry allows both condensation and expansion of subject matter in a way that conversational speech does not. These poems articulate some of the objective and subjective truths embodied in healing and change.

# ACKNOWLEDGMENTS

Writing for publication is a group effort. There are many who deserve thanks. My beloveds, Elizabeth and Sarah, provided much appreciated encouragement and support during the writing of this book. Loving thanks to my husband, Allen, for his enthusiasm about the book and general attentiveness to me throughout the process of writing it. I am grateful to him for sharing his exceptional ability to apply critical thinking to a creative process. I am thankful to Rosemerry Wahtola Trommer for her giving, supportive spirit and for connecting me to publishing resources. Pamela Warren Williams of Mercury HeartLink Press generously educated and ushered me as I navigated my way toward publication. Sheil Seclearr provided valuable editorial direction. I am grateful to Denise Weaver Ross for contributing her expertise in formatting and cover design.

Finally, I want to thank my patients. They are the collective core of this book. I would not have been able to write it without their willingness to bare their hearts and minds and souls. They have fueled my personal growth and maturation over the years and inspired my commitment to persevering and overcoming. I am grateful to all of them.

# CONTENTS

I am ready to say hello

I can't see myself

I am afraid of what's next

Are we in calm waters?

In the silence with you

I am present with you in the darkness

Do you have a magic wand?

How do you know my pain?

It feels good to be known by you

Can I attach?

I think I depend on you too much

Two steps forward, one step back

I am fine, and I am not fine

I am afraid to know my feelings

I grew up with devils and angels

I am grateful for them

Late for 10 am session

Does he care about me?

I love/hate my mother

How do you grow up without feelings?

Where do forbidden thoughts and feelings go?

My father was there, and he wasn't

I need my father

What's wrong with being average?

My sister betrayed me

Saturday mornings with my brother

Memories of Saturday mornings with my brother

I had special days with Grandma

I have come into being

FOR ALLEN

## Overcoming

I see my pain reflected in your eyes —
pools of sadness and grief,
wells of anxiety,
rivers of rage.

And yet, there is a steady calmness
in your presence
messaging hope
beckoning change.

As if to say
stay the course.
You are in the process of
overcoming.

# INTRODUCTION

This book of poems gives voice to some themes and experiences that are, in my view, representative of the psychotherapy process. The poems offered are by no measure exhaustive of themes or disorders addressed in psychotherapy. Nor should they be perceived as outlining specific therapeutic protocol. The poems offer insight into challenges of the human condition and pathways for overcoming. They are a distillation of clinical phenomena that, under typical circumstances, could take weeks, months, or even years to manifest in psychotherapy. The subject matter of psychotherapy can be disturbing, conflictual, emotionally painful, dark. I have not lightened the material in writing these poems. Rather, I have tried to present the subject matter so as to honor its authenticity. That is, to honor the rawness and complexity that characterizes the journey of psychotherapy. Similarly, I have tried to create poems that express the profound positive change and personal growth that psychotherapy can produce.

The reader may notice there are blank pages in the book. This formatting is purposeful. Psychotherapy sessions are surrounded by varying amounts of time and space. Both allow for additional taking in or internalization of the work done in session. In this book, blank space is juxtaposed with printed poems to encourage reflection and mental or emotional accommodation.

The book may be of interest to anyone who is curious about psychotherapy, about how identifying, expressing, and working through feelings can translate into improvement in well-being. The author's commentary, which accompanies many of the poems, may be of general interest to those who wonder how interpersonal dynamics "play out" in psychotherapy. The book provides an experiential gestalt of the nature of depth psychotherapy and may be of particular interest to students of psychology, lecturers and teachers seeking to educate about the process of growth and change, and early career psychotherapists and mental health professionals.

The poems are, in general, written from the patient's point of view with the therapist's words in italics. The poems do not contain actual transcribed material from real sessions. They offer a sense of being in the room and in the mind and heart of both the patient and the therapist. They are an homage to the beauty and rhythm and effort that characterize a therapeutic relationship.

# ONE ~ BEGINNING

The greatest compliment that was ever paid me was when one asked me what I thought, and attended to my answer.

*Henry David Thoreau*

*The first session and initial hours of psychotherapy are their own phenomenon. There is a lot at stake. The barrier to entering through the door of a psychotherapist's office is, in most cases, high. People tend to come when the emotional pain and conflict of living exceed the countering need to resist getting help, i.e., to expose oneself. Even those who easily bare themselves for exploration sometimes do so to hide underlying conflict and emotional pain. Sifting through the volume of information presented during a first session is demanding. Sometimes metaphors are useful to ground a budding relationship in a vision or understanding that can be jointly shared.*

I AM READY TO SAY HELLO

What should I talk about?

*Yourself.*

I was born...
I was raised...
My mother...
My father...
My friends...
My lover...
Now...
I want to believe that my life has been good and happy.

*And yet it sounds like it has not.*
*There has been a lot of emotional challenge.*

How could this be so?
That I've not been aware
of what life is for me.

*The heart lives in its own chambers.*
*It knows what it knows.*
*But the mind does not learn what the heart knows*
*until we are ready to see.*

4   BEGINNING

I CAN'T SEE MYSELF

My vision has been cloudy for so long.

*What is it that you have not seen clearly?*

That I have been in pain for a long time,
   sad about things I didn't know I was sad about,
   shredded up from grief,
   torn apart from anger,
   trying to wrap a blanket around me for comfort
   only it is full of holes.

*We can gather the shreds and torn pieces.*
*We can weave a blanket without holes.*
*Then you can see how beautiful it is.*

*After taking that first courageous step through the therapist's door, what follows is a process similar to a dance. Steps accumulate into patterns ranging from straightforward to complex, overt to covert, intentional to unintentional. At this stage, people sometimes want to be told what to talk about despite being encouraged to say whatever comes to mind. It can take some time to trust that it is safe to speak freely.*

I AM AFRAID OF WHAT'S NEXT

I'm not sure what to talk about today.
Last week I told you all about my sadness and inner turmoil.

*What comes to mind about that today?*

Ask me something and I will tell you.

*Tell me a little more and I will know better what to ask you.*

Tell you about my anxiety?

*Ok*

This lack of direction from you is making me anxious.

*How so?*

Again, you're not giving me guidance.

*Speak about what comes to mind, and I will find
a helpful direction.*

I'm not good at this.

*There is no good or bad or right or wrong.
I will listen without judgment and follow your lead.*

I want to be where there is no turmoil and tension.

*We can be together in the calm and quiet here.*

That is all that feels safe for now.

ARE WE IN CALM WATERS?

I felt such relief after last session.

*Tell me about your relief.*

It's like I can exhale. I've been holding all that in,
    all that we talked about.
What you said helped me think about things differently.
Only, now I realize there is a lot more to talk about.
I'm not sure where that will take me.
It feels good to have a place to sort it all out.
I can tell you are listening attentively.

*What do you most want me to hear?*

That I am strong but wounded. I want to be whole
    but don't know how to heal.

*I hear you. I see your strength and your wounds.*
*I must tell you, sometimes the pain gets worse before*
    *it gets better.*

So, it's not a smooth course from here?

*Turbulence ahead is likely.*
*It happens when redirecting life's flow.*

*Some people find the requirement to talk about themselves unappealing or uncomfortable. In fact, they may have trouble talking at all and be prone to silence and long pauses. In the silence, there is a whole world of inner thoughts and feelings, both conscious and not. Silence can hold anger, love, fear—a whole range of emotions juggling for expression or suppression.*

IN THE SILENCE WITH YOU

It is pleasant here with you.
Your presence is calming.
I feel a lot inside me.
I'm torn between talking and being quiet.
If I could just rest here all day with you I would.
I want to speak but feel I can't.

*Is there one word that comes to mind?*

Unsettled.

*What is unsettling?*

Everything. It's like that feeling before you're going to vomit.
You know it's coming and you can't stop it.
But you want to. You want to get back to when you felt better.

*I'm thinking about how you feel better after you've gotten it
all out.*

I prefer to keep things in.

I AM PRESENT WITH YOU IN THE DARKNESS

Don't you know that I am alone? Hopeless and desperate?
There is no way out.
I am surrounded, encaged — enraged.
NO, sunken into a black hole that is bottomless.

*I am present with you in the darkness.*

I'm terrified. There is only a sense of distance and aloneness.
I am seething with rage and desperate to express it.
But there is no point in uttering words.
I am riddled with fear, longing to assuage it,
   longing to find the key that will bring release.
I do not have hope.

*You are here, and I am with you.*
*I am on solid ground. You can join me.*
*Together, we can see light.*

*Some people remain in a dark place and are resistant to talking things through for some time. Others have a fantasy that the therapist will somehow magically fix them.*

DO YOU HAVE A MAGIC WAND?

If I come to see you every week,
    can you make it go away?
It keeps me from being happy.
It is so exhausting, consuming.
It takes up so much of my time and energy.
I am never really away from it.
I want you to help me with it.

*First, we must understand it.*

I wish you had a magic wand to make it better.
I'd hoped you could fix it.
I am in so much pain.
I don't know how to get rid of it.

*You want to believe that I can make all your pain go away.*

But you can't.

*Not on my own.*
*We can face your pain and work on it together.*

How do we start?
There is so much work to do.

*We have started. This is the work—*
    *talking about the pain.*

*Some patients are incredulous as they come to know a consistent, insightful, caring, attentive presence from the therapist. They sense a phenomenon at play, something exceptional that may not be fully explained by the therapist's years of professional education and training.*

# How do you know my pain?

How do you know what you know about me?
Where do the wells of empathy come from?
How can your insight be so consistently accurate
   as if you are living in my head?

*There is no greater teacher than the self.*
*And in order to sit here, in the therapist's chair,*
   *one needs to have sat there, on the patient couch.*

*It is not that I have been in your shoes.*
*I have been in my shoes, limping from scars.*
*And I recognize when others are limping.*
*I know what it takes to heal and strengthen,*
   *to learn to walk in comfort.*

*I am very familiar with the journey.*

# Two ~ AS THERAPY PROGRESSES

The fact that grief takes so long to resolve is not a sign of
inadequacy but betokens depth of soul.

*Donald Woods Winnicott*

*When trust in the therapist increases, usually motivation to self-disclose follows. Allowing oneself to speak freely without judgment allows the inner private self to emerge and be seen and, eventually, be known.*

IT FEELS GOOD TO BE KNOWN BY YOU

I go on and on, session after session.
Your patience with me is remarkable.

*What would make me impatient with you?*

Nothing it seems. Your attention is unwavering.

*Perhaps you are worth listening to.*

I'm beginning to feel this is true.
At first, I did not expect to be heard or taken seriously.
There are so many others with problems worse than mine.

*That does not change your problems.*
*Your talking allows me to know you.*

To be heard,
   to be seen,
   to be known,
   is helpful.

*These things matter.*
*You matter.*

*While some individuals enter psychotherapy with a longing to be known and seen and heard, others come with fears about connection or an inability to experience attachment. The therapist's consistent interest, attention, and availability create the environment, the emotional space, in which relational connection can develop.*

## CAN I ATTACH?

There is disorder in my head.
 I'm always thinking,
   "on the one hand"
   "on the other hand"
I can't settle into myself,
   into a space
   where my thoughts are not riddled with doubt.
Or a space
   where I don't worry
    about what others are thinking or expecting.

*It's hard to feel secure.*

I only know insecurity—
   the sense that there is no place
   where I am ok.

*How do you feel here with me?*

Well, you're very professional, interested.
You're teaching me to pay attention to myself.

*How is that?*

You pay attention to me.
I can count on it.

*How does it feel to have my full attention?*

On the one hand...
On the other hand...

*Those are your thoughts.*
*I'm curious how my*
*undivided attention feels to you.*

Nice, I suppose.

*You suppose?*

It's hard to feel that I matter.
It's hard to feel attached to you.

*What's hard about it?*

I just don't... I can't...
I'm changing the subject now.

*To what?*

Doesn't matter. Anything.

*Anything else but letting yourself feel secure here with me.*

I'm trying.

*I'm here. You can reach out for me.*

I THINK I DEPEND ON YOU TOO MUCH

I am starting to fear that I depend on you too much.

*What frightens you about depending on me?*

It is not safe.
I might get hurt.
You might reject me.
I might reject you.
That might hurt you.
Because I know you care about me.
I care about you.
If I just don't get too close, too dependent...

*Then what?*

I will be alone and back where I started.

*Then what?*

I will be hurt and needy,
   anxious, and angry.

*Maybe attachment can be good and safe.*
*Maybe it can mean you are dependent in a healthy way.*

Like letting myself need someone without worrying about it?

*Yes*

Can I do that with you?

*Yes*

*Therapy does not progress in a linear fashion. There are sessions that feel like treading water. There are occasional "breakthrough" sessions where an impactful insight shifts perspective to allow a whole new view of the self and the world. But it is customary to move forward and then regress. As long as moving forward occurs in greater frequency and magnitude than regression, there is progress.*

TWO STEPS FORWARD, ONE STEP BACK

I've been feeling good about things.

But last week
I flew into a rage, like the old days.
I felt tired and frustrated and uncertain about myself.
Something inconsequential set me off.
I guess I needed to be angry.
Somehow it felt safer than being content.
Content. Settled. Confident. Happy.
These are unfamiliar to me.

A few days ago
I was recognized for my outstanding contribution to a project
at work.
That felt good.

Yesterday
I yelled at my kid for no good reason when he asked me to
go to the park.
I felt strangely unsettled.
Sometimes it is hard to believe he actually wants to be with
me.

Today
I kissed my partner tenderly before leaving for the day.
We both enjoyed the intimacy.
That feels good.

*One of the challenges of psychotherapy is unmasking.*
*That is, to demonstrate straightforward authenticity. Instead,*
*people can be motivated to hide unwanted or unacceptable*
*underlying feelings with a presentation that does not match*
*how they feel inside. Those who struggle in this way can*
*vacillate between feeling good and bad about themselves.*

I AM FINE, AND I AM NOT FINE

I am fine. I am good.
I am principled.
I am capable.
I am likeable and kind.

WAIT...

I am not fine.
There is deception in me that masks my internal truths
    and beliefs.
I deceive others also.

At times, defiance simmers in me just below the surface,
    hovering on top of boiling resentment.
How dare you disregard me!!
How could you abandon me?

WAIT...

How could you love me?
I am unworthy.
I am incompetent.
I am loathsome.
I am not fine.

*Some people manage conflict or threatening thoughts and feelings by compartmentalization. This is analogous to putting things away in a box that one doesn't want to face or address. The box is then kept out of sight. Opening the box and addressing what's inside can be very threatening.*

I AM AFRAID TO KNOW MY FEELINGS

On the surface, I live and work and think and act.
Sometimes, I do not want to know what is below.

Below the surface, compartments contain things.

DREAMS
      NIGHTMARES
            MEMORIES
                WISHES
                      FORBIDDEN THINGS


*What will happen if you know what is below?*

I can't know about these things.

*What makes you believe this?*

It is not safe to feel in the darkness of below.

*What makes it unsafe?*

Injury, harm, destruction.

*People who experience abusive relationships can be motivated and able to survive these with the help of other relationships that are emotionally and behaviorally healthy. These relationships may provide intermittent or continuous mitigating influences that help counter abusive experiences. In addition, these relationships may be viewed as a lifeline, a source of reparation and well-being.*

I GREW UP WITH DEVILS AND ANGELS

I was raised by a devil—
   cold,
   evil,
   abusive.

What I hoped was warmth became
   fiery rage, criticism, rejection.

Despite this I somehow survived.

Occasionally, an angel would visit —
   warm,
   loving,
   guiding.

What I feared would be harmful proved
   comforting, supportive, nourishing.

Because of this I wanted to survive.

I AM GRATEFUL FOR THEM

It's because of you that I can breathe and be.
I know the warmth of embrace and the pleasure of gentle
    caress from you.
I'm motivated to be in the world—do something productive,
    rewarding.
I even have relationships that are worth something.
You treated me like I was worth something.
You are my rock—undamaged by battering forces
    of destruction.
You sheltered me from destruction.
I am so grateful.

*Boundaries, by definition, indicate the limit or edge of something. Some people easily accept the necessity of boundaries for optimal safety and functioning in life. Others challenge boundaries because of conscious or unconscious conflict in connection with the dividing lines boundaries impose. How one manages the boundary of time in psychotherapy can provide a bounty of information about the self to be usefully observed and explored.*

## LATE FOR 10 AM SESSION

I want to be with you. I am excited to see you.
I feel better after our session.
I have mixed feelings about the effort and time and money
   it takes to see you.
Maybe you have mixed feelings about me.
Maybe you will refuse to see me if I am late.
Maybe I am special to you...your favorite.
So, you will be very disappointed if I arrive late.
Maybe it will make you angry if I am late...so angry
   that you lose control.
Then, I will be in danger when I arrive.
I am used to being in danger.
Maybe you will feel disrespected when I arrive late.
And I will be ashamed and regret behaving badly.
You cannot force me to arrive at a certain time.
You do not control me.

10:10

I'm here.

*I'm here.*

*At their core, people want to be treated respectfully, to know that their feelings matter and will be meaningfully addressed. In a relationship, people can express love differently and get upset about different things even though what both want and need is quite aligned.*

## DOES HE CARE ABOUT ME?

I am tormented by wanting what I cannot have.
Doesn't he know that I need attention, support, understanding?
Instead, he reacts aggressively to my pain and rallies to try to
   fix the problem, swearing, foul-mouthed, angry, agitated,
   like a soldier ready to do battle.

*It seems he is ready to go to battle for you.*
*Would you rather he retreat into passive indifference?*

I would like him to hold me tight, to comfort and soothe me
   with words and touch.

*These are not his natural skills. He has learned to show love*
   *through action.*
*He reacts to defend himself and those he loves.*

He acts like my pain is about him.

*Is it not? When you are threatened or hurt by another,*
   *this also impacts him.*

He is defensive and over-reactive. I can't deal with it.

*I wonder if you already identified how you can.*

Can what?

*Deal with it.*
*You are soothed by thoughtful words,*
   *supportive understanding,*
   *comforting touch.*

We both need this to feel better and be ok?

*What soothes you may soothe him.*

Who goes first? Who soothes whom first?

*There is no rule, no one right way.*

To get what I need, I must give him what I need.

*Sometimes.*

# THREE ~ FAMILY MATTERS

A good life is like a weaving. Energy is created in the tension.
The struggle, the pull and tug are everything.

*Joan Erikson*

*Many hours in depth psychotherapy can be devoted to exploration of relationships from childhood, particularly with one's primary caretakers. The characteristics and nature of early relationships can impact identity formation and maturational issues well into adult life. These impacts can be profoundly negative or positive and often amplify over the course of one's life.*

I LOVE/HATE MY MOTHER

I loved her so.
But she could not receive my love.
She didn't recognize my efforts to make her proud,
    to make her notice me,
    to make her care.
Absorbed in her own aggrandizement,
    worried about diminishment,
    nothing ever satisfied her.
Now, she is old and powerless over me.
I have found my way without her guidance.
Sometimes I still see her in her home.
I get a creepy, crawly feeling.
She is like a crustacean: a creature with hardened exterior,
    still somewhat comely under the right lighting,
    yet without inner strength — no spine.
And the antennae are still out searching for what she can
    extract for herself from the universe.

*It is common for children of self-involved or emotionally unavailable parents to struggle with anger and resentment about this in adulthood. Patients are aware that their emotional development and capacity for healthy expression and assertion have been muted in association with inadequate or dismissive parenting.*

HOW DO YOU GROW UP WITHOUT FEELINGS?

She was not a good mother.
Not even good enough.
She focused on her needs.
I was her proxy.
For her purposes
I behaved as she wanted and needed me to behave.
I knew no other way to get her attention or approval.
My needs were rarely in the equation, or even on the radar.
My feelings were dismissed with blanket categorizations.
"You are too sensitive." "You think too much about things."

How is a child supposed to become an independent,
   functional adult if she doesn't feel and think?

*She can't.*

WHERE DO FORBIDDEN THOUGHTS AND FEELINGS GO?

Where do the thoughts and feelings go?
The ones I'm not supposed to have, not allowed to have,
   not able to have?
They can't just evaporate, disappear.
Where do they live?

*Well...denial, avoidance, disconnection, drugs, drama, acting out,*
   *anxiety, insomnia, addictions, depression, shame, and so on.*
*Unexpressed feelings find a home in these places.*

*They live in better places too.*
*They live in dreams, hopes, ambitions, goals, relationships.*
*Here the self-affirmations and also taboos survive.*

They are all mixed together then...
   the good, the bad, the ugly, and the wonderful?

*They hide in plain sight, noticeable to anyone who wants to see.*

*Parental passivity or inconsistency can impact development of effective life management skills. It is common to feel confusion, frustration, or sadness when relating to a parent who, in some ways, functions as expected and, in some ways, does not.*

## My father was there, and he wasn't

I see now that he was a passive man.
Many thought he was agreeable,
   always willing to go along with what others wanted.
But he was just passively obliging.
It got the best of him over time.
Worn and weary from decades of complacency, in his later
   years, he told me he'd lost all interest in life.
What possessed him to allow this outcome?
He seemed like a man of principle.
He worked. He provided. He was generous.
   At times, he was playful.
But mostly, he was passive.
He made decisions by choosing the path of least resistance.
He did not speak clearly about his opinions and frequently
   denied having feelings.
In fact, his refusal to acknowledge emotion frustrated others
   to the point of exasperation.
Perhaps that was the clearest form of communication he
   could muster.
Caught in the circularity of hopes and dreams rising
   only to be snuffed out by differing needs of others,
   he chose to rattle some chains before retreating into passivity.
The cycle repeated endlessly.
It was safe and predictable and required little from him
   beyond compliance.
I wonder. Was there no better way for him?

# I NEED MY FATHER

He was strict and stern. I don't ever recall him telling me
  he loved me.
He had a strong work ethic
  and demanded productivity of himself and others.
He saw himself as a man with integrity
  giving time and attention to causes he favored.
When I turned 18, or was it 21, he said he was done
  parenting me.
After grappling with my puzzlement, I determined that
  he wanted to be free from the burdening responsibilities of
  my hopes and needs.
I accepted this shove toward independence.
But it came with a price.
I grew to believe that my hopes and needs could no longer
  be prioritized.
I feel duty-bound to accommodate others
  to concern myself routinely with the welfare of others
  to make certain I am not the source of others' suffering.
I think my father's announcement, decidedly pragmatic,
  was the way for him to shift our relationship
  from father-child to father-adult child.
The announcement implied that I was free to live
  according to my own devices.
And so was he.
Still, I need my father.

*While some individuals struggle with conflict arising from emotionally absent or disengaged parents, others struggle to reconcile mixed feelings about parental expectations and involvements that are excessive.*

WHAT'S WRONG WITH BEING AVERAGE?

My parents are amazing
and intense.
They offer support and encouragement
that has no bounds.
I appreciate this and also feel burdened by it.
There is an implied expectation
that I will become a fabulous, outstanding person
because they have given me so much...
of everything.
I feel guilty when I recognize our differences.
I know they want me to thrive,
but sometimes I just want to be average.
Why can't it be good enough to be good enough?
Am I not loveable the way I am?

*Siblings can play significant roles in either exacerbating or providing refuge from family dysfunction. Also, a sibling who is by nature, or who is perceived to be, an outlier in the family system can be a target for disregard and other types of rejections.*

## MY SISTER BETRAYED ME

She stood there while our father accused me
  and she allowed me to be blamed.
She saw my confusion. She saw my utter helplessness
  as I tried to get Dad to believe in my innocence.
Defeated, I was punished for the dent in his car.
I did not know my sister was the guilty one, but I suspected her.
Years later, my sister confessed.
Dad laughed while apologizing to me.
He said, at the time of the incident, I seemed so nervous.
He assumed this was indication of my guilt.
It was not a real apology.
At the time of the incident, I WAS nervous.
I felt entrapped,
  sensing the inevitability of being scapegoated.
It frequently went that way between us growing up.
Sister was just like Dad and
  neither of them could be bothered to see the truth about me.

*There is a wide range of sibling behavior that is normal and healthy and can include typical sparring and jockeying for attention or approval. Abusive sibling relationships are characterized by an imbalance of power in which one sibling feels a degree of helplessness with no recourse to address a conflictual situation.*

## SATURDAY MORNINGS WITH MY BROTHER

I looked out the window watching as Mom drove away in her car.
She left this same time every Saturday to do errands.
My brother was the babysitter.
It started out as brothers wrestling and rough housing.
But then it became something else.
It felt exciting and dangerous and good and bad all at the
    same time.
My brother told me we should not talk with Mom about our
    wrestling time.
I sort of worshipped my brother.
He always had friends asking him over to do cool stuff.
At least, that's what I thought.
I thought he must be doing really cool, interesting stuff with
    his friends.
Because he never wanted me to come along.
He never wanted me around except on Saturday mornings.
We never spoke about it as we got older.
At some point, he stopped babysitting me.
I've never spoken about it with anyone.
It's weird. He was the older one, you know, the one looking
    after me supposedly.
But I feel ashamed.

MEMORIES OF SATURDAY MORNINGS WITH MY BROTHER

I am ashamed of what I felt.

*What did you feel?*

I liked the stimulation, the sexual eroticism of it all.
But those are not feelings to have with that person.

*What person?*

My brother.

*It is natural to be aroused when stimulated. If this happens too soon, before normal curiosity about sexual behavior has occurred, it can trigger an overwhelming mix of good and bad feelings.*

Why do I feel ashamed?

*Describe the shame.*

There is a sense of humiliation. I knew it was not right, what we were doing, but I felt helpless to stop it.

*How could you have stopped it?*

I couldn't. I tried to at first, but he was ignoring me, telling me to stop being a prissy, laughing at me like it was stupid to be upset. I felt like I didn't understand and, somehow, he knew better. Now, I feel foolish that I ever thought that.

*You were in an impossible situation, a situation you did not have the maturity to understand nor the skills to confront.*

It is still unsettled between us.

*I can help you confront it now.*

How will that help?

*It will change the feeling that you did nothing and help you feel in control.*

*Some individuals have a surrogate, a non-parent, who provides invaluable nurturance that has a life-long positive influence. This nurturance may be consciously taken in and productively used throughout early development and into adulthood. Alternatively, this nurturance may be held in waiting, or in secret, to be called upon when it is safe to do so.*

## I HAD SPECIAL DAYS WITH GRANDMA

Sometimes Grandma and I walked in the woods behind
   her house.
On special days we went to the stream where wild orchids
   grew along the edge.
Grandma called the orchids "Lady's Slippers."
It took me a while to see the resemblance.
But I understood her words immediately.
She told me this was a most beautiful flower.
She said it had an appealing delicacy
   and also strength to provide protection from
   harsh conditions.
Grandma had a way of showing her feelings
   and describing them at the same time.
I particularly relished her words on this occasion.
I knew she was teaching me about myself.
It was a beautiful lesson.
For several springs in a row, Grandma took me
   to the wild orchids.

I HAVE COME INTO BEING

The seeds of self survived
   while I was folded into her bosom, almost smothered,
   attuned to her relentless rhythms, her moods, her
   expectations of me.
I protected myself, sometimes aware of this, sometimes not.
My conflict became headaches or stomach aches
   or sleeplessness or fear of the dark
   or fear of being with others or fear of being left alone
   or fear of getting attention when I knew she wanted attention
   or fear of needing things when I knew she needed things.
It was confusing. Then it was angering.
Then I felt helpless to do anything with the fear or the anger
   because she was always there needing, demanding so
   much from me.
Still...I did feel and think and want and need.
I kept the seeds of self protected, intact,
   until it was safe to be nurtured, to develop, to mature.
It has been safe for some time now.
I have blossomed.
I have come into being.

# Four ~ DARKNESS INTO LIGHT

Once we believe in ourselves, we can risk curiosity, wonder, spontaneous delight, or any experience that reveals the human spirit.

*e e cummings*

*Human nature and functioning are complex and elude straightforward understanding. Conscious and unconscious motivations and actions produce unanticipated realities or unwanted truths. Choices made at one point in life can shift into negative territory during a different life stage. Despondency, depression, hopelessness can manifest when the entanglements of life choices appear inescapable. Finding a way forward requires acceptance, forgiveness, and courage.*

# How do I get out of this bind?

This agony, this bind is relentless.
My choices have led to an outcome that is unacceptable to me,
and I can't change it.

*What do you want to be different?*

I want to go back and choose a different life path.

*What is unacceptable about the path you are on?*

I am not loved or fulfilled or happy.

*What can you do about that?*

There is no way out. I feel helpless.

*Choices can have consequences we do not expect or want.*
*The clarity of hindsight can both wound and soothe.*

There is nothing soothing about realizing I made life decisions
that I regret.

*Accepting the truth frees you from the blindness of denial.*
*That is something.*

It is not enough.

*No, it's the beginning of a different vision.*
*In this vision, you see*
*that you made the best choices you could*
*under the circumstances.*
*You see that your circumstances have changed.*

*You forgive yourself for making mistakes, some serious. You recognize that acceptance and forgiveness are salves for injuries we did not prevent or cannot escape.*

*And courageously, you choose to step forward.*

*Certain conditions in psychotherapy result in the development of idealization. This is a process in which one assigns sweeping positive attributions to the therapist that are unrealistic. Idealization can be both satisfying and confusing and is sometimes equated with being in love. This is a tricky situation. When handled with straightforwardness and sensitivity, these intense positive feelings usually progress to a more balanced and productive understanding of the psychotherapeutic relationship.*

## ARE WE IN LOVE?

I rely so much on you. I look forward to seeing you.
It is clear to me how much you care.
Never before have I been seen or understood so clearly.
You are so helpful to me.
I have changed for the better because of my time with you.
Sometimes I think this feels like love.

*It feels wonderful to be with me,*
   *to feel my attention and care and regard.*

You speak without declaring yourself.

*We have been on an intimate, meaningful journey together.*
*To say we are in love is complicated.*

Our relationship is unique to us.
It is real.
I can feel what I want about you.
I can sort of make you into what I need you to be.
You are there for me in ways that I need.
It feels genuine.

*I am genuinely fond of you.*

It's like you are a little in love with me, but not really.
Perhaps you are allowing me to love you.
Then, I can know what it feels like.
I am practicing here with you.
I am getting ready for someone else to be in love with me, truly.

*As therapy continues and the work deepens, there are sessions that include moments of profound joy. These result from the dedication of both patient and therapist to the psychotherapeutic process. There is shared perspective on what it has taken to arrive at a particular point of insight or change. These moments are deeply gratifying.*

JOYFUL

Sometimes there is joy...
  in the news that a long-suffering patient has found true love.
  in knowing that self-assertion can change the unattainable into
    the achievable.
  in the experience of connection that restores trust in the ability
    to love.
  in the awareness of inner darkness transforming to light.
  in knowing that one has survived and even thrives.
 Sometimes there is joy—resounding, transcending, triumphant.

Sometimes there is joy...
  in the news that a foe has offered an olive branch.
  in knowing one is now capable of loving and being.
  in the experience of honoring self.
  in the awareness of calm where anxiety used to live and reign.
  in knowing what one knows: hard stop.
  Sometimes there is joy—quiet, enveloping.

## WE ARE GETTING IT FIGURED OUT

When I started, I had no words.
Feelings, thoughts, memories, roiling on the surface
　　intersected with fears, anger, sadness, shame
　　swirling underneath.
With you, exploration and understanding educate and
　　fortify me.
Speaking and listening prompt me to find and use my words.
I carry my words with me now like a reference book.
This resource is available to me at any time.
I need only reference self-knowing when choosing to speak.
Confidently, I claim my opinions.
When I am uncertain or don't know,
　　I can defer with humility.
Differing views and understandings no longer threaten me.
There is room, graciously, respectfully, for me.

*Later-stage depth psychotherapy focuses increasingly on identifying and working through personal contribution to negative and positive life outcomes. This is the stage when taking responsibility for change, growth, and functional self-management is most likely and possible. Increased self-understanding and relational capacity shift perspective and behavior. Often, this brings fulfillment and relief.*

## Are we done yet?

Are we done yet?
I have learned about myself.
I've learned about how my past contributes to my present.
My perspectives have shifted.

*In what ways?*

I see how I contribute to my relationship difficulties,
my anxiety, my depression,
my lack of career advancement.

*How do you contribute?*

I can be distant, irritable, unmotivated,
see the glass as half empty.

*What is that about?*

It is about my past, my mother, my father, my family, my boss.

*We are not done yet.*

AGAIN, ARE WE DONE YET?

Are we done yet?
I have learned about myself.
I've learned about how my past contributes to my present.
My perspectives have shifted.

*In what ways?*

I see how I contribute to my relationship difficulties,
my anxiety, my depression,
my lack of career advancement.

*How do you contribute?*

I can be distant, irritable, unmotivated,
see the glass as half empty.

*What is that about?*

I learned to be distant and unmotivated
    because I was afraid I would not be taken seriously.
That made me angry.
I felt there was no point in trying.

*Your life conditions are different now.*

I can sometimes see the glass is half full.
I am impacted by issues from the past
    but I've learned how to take myself seriously.
I've learned how to let others love me.
I am responsible for that.

*Yes, we are almost done.*

*Near the end of psychotherapy, patients are able to identify what outcomes are desirable or possible and what limitations are inherent in life's course.*

## My own person

Years have been devoted to expectations of me,
    to responsibilities of adulthood,
    to competition with peers,
    to internal standards of success.
The irony is that nothing fully satisfies.
I am most content when I am alone.
I want to want to be with others
    but I do not.

*You enjoy being here with me.*

You expect nothing of me, nothing that is burdensome.

*What do I expect that you enjoy?*

You expect me to speak freely,
    to identify feelings, needs, desires, expectations.
You encourage me to find a path to fulfillment.

*You could act on all that outside of here.*
*What would that be like?*

Like exhaling as I propel forward,
    moving toward others, toward life.
Still, I will enjoy being alone,
    being my own person,
    choosing how to engage, how to connect.

*A good plan for yourself of your own devising.*

I AM NOW RESPONSIBLE

Blame is so easily cast.
Horrible, hurtful things happen.
And then there is salt in the wound
   when the offender does not make amends.
I did not deserve the treatment I received,
   the inflicted wounds.
And yet, these things happened.
I cannot change what occurred.
If I do not choose to heal, forgive, look from a different view,
   I will live with open wounds.
I am responsible for the life that is healing,
   for conditions that allow scar formation.
My scars will remind me of past wounds,
   wounds that no longer fester,
   but have healed
   from courage and strength within.

*Increasing functionality paired with improvement or resolution of difficulties present at the beginning of therapy stir thoughts and feelings about stopping therapy. This is another opportunity for personal growth. Therapy ends with the duality of literal separation from the therapist and an emotional bond that is enduring.*

I THINK IT'S TIME TO GO

I find myself thinking about stopping.
It occurs to me that I am handling things well.
The writhing and bleeding stopped long ago.
The journey from that point to the present has taught me
   to look outward
   and trust inward.
Signs of healing appear after the process has already begun.
Internal change drives what is external.
The challenge is in paying attention,
   conscious, disciplined, continuous attention.
This taught me how and when to act.
I have learned that acting in my best interest also benefits
   others.
I can do this now.
It is wonderful to know what I want and get it,
   not because I am entitled. Because I am enabled.
Pleasure is not elusive.
My enjoyment stirs others
   to enjoy themselves and me.
Increasingly, I am attentive, often to others.
This mirrors my increased capacity to attend to myself,
   to be me.

## You are with me always

You are a part of me now.
I will no longer be with you in this space,
   no longer see you and talk to you
   or hear your voice and words.
I am not concerned about this because I carry you inside.
I know what you would say,
   what you would offer to me that would be helpful.
Now, I can say and offer these things to myself.
It comes easily, sometimes automatically,
   replacing the defaults I used to depend on that did not
   serve me well.
You are timelessly embedded.
There is no worry about expiration or obsolescence.
I no longer need you.
You are with me.

# About the Author

Diana Bowling is a clinical psychologist in Denver, CO. She has been treating individuals with a range of human conflicts and disorders for over 30 years as well as providing clinical consultation and supervision. Dr. Bowling was inspired to write about psychotherapy in poetic form to articulate and share some truths about the nature of conflict and change. She is frequently asked about what happens in psychodynamic psychotherapy and how it works. Poems are a medium in which the complexity and nuance of working through emotional pain and working toward change can be expressed. Her writing is an homage to the beauty, rhythm, and effort that characterize a healing relationship.

Dr. Bowling has an MS in Developmental Psychology from Columbia University and a PhD in Clinical Psychology from the California School of Professional Psychology. She was a Clinical Fellow in the Medical Department at MIT. After decades of clinical practice, she recently returned to a focus on writing and literature which were her early career interests during her undergraduate years at Smith College. This is her first book of poetry.

Made in the USA
Monee, IL
05 December 2021

84010232R00068